VANISHING POINTS

POEMS

GARY METRAS

DOS MADRES

2021

DOS MADRES PRESS INC.
P.O. Box 294, Loveland, Ohio 45140
www.dosmadres.com   editor@dosmadres.com

Dos Madres is dedicated to the belief that the small press is essential to the vitality of contemporary literature as a carrier of the new voice, as well as the older, sometimes forgotten voices of the past. And in an ever more virtual world, to the creation of fine books pleasing to the eye and hand.

Dos Madres is named in honor of Vera Murphy and Libbie Hughes, the "Dos Madres" whose contributions have made this press possible.

Dos Madres Press, Inc. is an Ohio Not For Profit Corporation and a 501 (c) (3) qualified public charity. Contributions are tax deductible.

Executive Editor: Robert J. Murphy

Illustration & Book Design: Elizabeth H. Murphy
www.illusionstudios.net

Typeset in Adobe Garamond Pro & Goudy Old Style
ISBN 978-1-953252-42-5
Library of Congress Control Number: 2021946500

First Edition
Copyright 2021 Gary Metras

Published by Dos Madres Press, Inc.

Talking River Review: "The Wine Glass"
Tar Wolf Review: "Islands of Farewell"
Tears In The Fence (UK): "The Girl on the Cover of the
      Magazine"
The American Voice: "Straight Lines"
Third Wednesday: "Everywhere at Once"
Wild Earth: "Winter Temperatures"
Yarrow: "Narrating the Pond's Night"

"Anonymous Donation" appeared in the author's chapbook,
      The Yearnings, Samisdat Press, and is reprinted in the
      anthology *Working Words: Punching the Clock and
      Kicking Out the Jams*, Coffee House Press.
"Hamlet as Anthroapologist" and "Lint" appeared in the
      author's chapbook, *Today's Lesson*, Bull Thistle Press.
"Lint" appeared in the author's chapbook *Greatest Hits 1980-
      2006*, Pudding House, and in *American Life in Poetry*,
      ed. Ted Kooser.
"The Flame" included in *Poetry Oracle: Elemental Inspirations*,
      SoulPathSanctuary
"Vanishing Point" reprinted in the anthology, *Passionate Hearts*,
      New World Library.

ACKNOWLEDGEMENTS

Art:Mag: "A Summary of Love Letters Never Mailed"
The Bellingham Review: "Vanishing Point"
Calapooya: "This Life" (under the title "This Is")
Dark Horse: "Anonymous Donation"
Embers: "Approaching Harvest"
En Passant: "Parable of the Fish"
Forge: "The Promise of Song"
Heavy Bear: "In the Cellar," "The Ghost of Love: A Valentine of
    Loss"
High Rock Review: "Another Winter"
Hiram Poetry Review: "Early Ice"
Istanbul Literary Review: "Prince Rupert of Bavaria Stands atop
    a Wall of Castle d'Coucy 1917," "Troubled"
Longhouse Reader: "Lint"
Lungfish Review: "Dance of the Night Hawks," "Hamlet as
    Anthroapologist"
Main Street Rag: "Molasses Cookies"
Muddy River Poetry Review: "Mapping the Heart"
Negative Capability: "The Birth," "Prayer in Autumn"
North Dakota Quarterly: "The Flame"
Northern Pleasure: "The Last Childhood Hero"
One Art: A Journal of Poetry: "At the Nursing Home"
One Trick Pony: "History and Oxymorons"
Peregrine: "Urania," "Song of the Coming and Going," "Love:
    The Unspoken"
Poetic Justice: "Adam, Returning"
Poetry East: "An Old Story," "Lint"
Poets On: "Beached Whale," "First Spring"
Potato Eyes: "Modern Farm"
Presa: "Cold as Omen"
Santa Fe Literary Review: "Engineering Sweet Dreams"
Stone Country: "Concerto for Love: A Night Piece"

for Natalie

CONTENTS

1

The Flame ... 1

Another Winter ... 2

Cold as Omen ... 4

Prince Rupert of Bavaria Stands
        atop a Wall of Castle d'Coucy 1917... 5

The Religion of Wine ... 6

Everywhere at Once ... 7

Urania ... 8

Parable of the Fish ... 9

In the Cellar ... 10

May 31, 2008 ... 11

Mapping the Heart ... 12

Bad Day ... 13

2

Approaching Harvest ... 17

The Promise of Song ... 18

Beached Whale ... 19

Song of the Coming and Going ... 22

Prayer in Autumn ... 23

Early Ice ... 24

Narrating the Pond's Night ... 25

Troubled ... 28

Two Views of the Apocalypse ... 29

Straight Lines ... 31

Winter Temperatures ... 32

Dance of the Night Hawks ... 33

3

Adam, Returning ... 37
History and Oxymorons ... 39
Hamlet as Anthroapologist ... 40
Molasses Cookies ... 41
At the Nursing Home ... 42
This Life ... 43
HIV ... 44
The Girl on the Cover of the Magazine ... 45
A House Without Chicken ... 46
Modern Farm ... 47
Anonymous Donation ... 48
Lint ... 49

4

The Wine Glass ... 53
Concerto for Love: A Night Piece ... 54
A Summary of Love Letters Never Mailed ... 55
The Ghost of Love: A Valentine of Loss ... 56
Islands of Farewell ... 60
The Last Childhood Hero ... 61
Love: The Unspoken ... 62
An Old Story ... 63
Vanishing Point ... 65
First Spring ... 66
The Birth ... 67
Engineering Sweet Dreams ... 70

About the Author... 73

1

THE FLAME

A candle burned on the table.
A candle burned.
　　—Pasternak, *Dr. Zhivago*

The moment plays
upon itself, repeating
in flames and shadows
on the wall,
flame and shadow,
where the world
is battered
to a house reduced
by hungry wind.
Wind and snow.
A white persistence
as unforgiving as night.
The horizon vanishes
from sleeping minds
but thin wisps
of bent trees sway
like flames against
the frozen sky. Exhausted
ashes fall. A sleeper
awakes and rises
to relight a candle
in the cold air.
Flame and shadow.
He stares and stares
into that flame.
A heart moves on the wall
like a shadow.

1

ANOTHER WINTER

Old Tom, mountain
beyond the backyard, sleeps
like a titan. For you
this is just another winter.
The snow numbs. The wind chafes.
Dream is your retreat.
The valley you sprang from
has been measured, marked, cut
and built on
as if there was nothing else
for men to do.
When the snow comes
where will those boundaries be?
Your flank was hacked out like a tumor
so we could ski in our health.
An antenna is your crown, blinking
the night long journey we think
will last eternity.
The scrub pine bend under snow.
You hardly flinch in your waiting,
in the deep mystery of your stone.
The land would be barren without
your height, like a boy
with no father, or man without God,
a monotony beyond us all.
When the snow melts, sluicing down
your wind sculpted side,
a few more trees will be cut,
a foundation or two
dug to gape with the emptiness

hopes are built from.
And then new neighbors,
who'll look at you
in June deliciousness and wonder
what to do with time,
while you attend all the winters
to come.

COLD AS OMEN

For Good-Night a cheek peck, mouths closed,
lips tight against a two-day cough sure to blossom
during this single-digit night. Snow rained on,
refrozen. You can walk atop it and not sink.

Not a miracle. But faith helps. As does good balance.
And sensible shoes. Even deer seeking nourishment
slip, fall, break a bone. Here, the weather is fine
under a down comforter. Yet that cough vibrating

the moonlit air, chilling the kiss before sleep, before
dream. Yes, the body has limits and the sleeping
mind heals even as the lungs constrict to feed
an esophagus of spasmodic explosions.

Wait, then gurgle water with a spoon of salt.
When you see a star shooting over an icy meadow,
kiss the person beside you, full, hot on the mouth.

PRINCE RUPERT OF BAVARIA STANDS
ATOP A WALL OF CASTLE D'COUCY 1917

Das Burgerbauen war scher immer unser Lust
—Günter Grass

Always, a neighbor's castle brings
envy and suspicion. Why do they need
such thick walls? Why so many
parapets, a watchman in each? We add
a higher tower to ours, deepen
the moat while aiming a howitzer
at their north wall. We'll build
a summer castle in the cool mountains
to secure the frontier, another to the west
where forest succumbs to desert.
Behind these walls we sleep
with one eye open.

THE RELIGION OF WINE

Melk, Austria

A thousand years the monks of Melk making wine.
Enough to get everyone in the village tipsy,
especially *das mädchen*. Generations
of sated men and pregnant girls, until the Pope
tore the Abbey down to save virtue, to salve
the guilt of fathers and daughters.
The Brothers? Scattered across Europe
with the secrets of grapevine, the harvest,
fermentation. So that throughout the empire
of God there was wine and its ceremonies
of pleasure. Then the Abbey rebuilt,
more beautiful than ever, carved columns,
intricate glass, painted ceilings, the second best
pipe organ in the realm, and ten shades
of grape, ten flavors of wine, enough to please
every palate, layman or clergy, virtuous and not . . .

EVERYWHERE AT ONCE

Massive clouds creep
over the mountain from the east—
the storm that formed
over North Carolina two days ago
has drifted out to sea,
missed us,
and is stalled over the Atlantic.

There will be no new snow
to cover the sand and road salt
staining the edges of streets
from last week's storm.
Today we face the world
as it is: rust, debris and small bones
beneath melting snow.

Gravity, alone,
can not do its job—
rain and mist
press us to the ground,
to the earthy crust that wants to rise
and drift out to sea,
to float and rise in air,

into the forgetfulness of winds
that whoop one minute
and sigh the next,
the winds whose home is nowhere
and everywhere at once,
the winds that ruffle the hair
of the man standing in the field
looking at clouds.

7

URANIA

"When you meet the Buddha, kill the Buddha"

On the path where he meets you
beneath the one tree
still leafed against the season,
your eyes question his arms.
Will he fold them around you,
or will he fill his hands
with the sad stones
that litter this ground,
hurl them and run in fear
to the brooding shadows?
Somewhere on this path
to the dry garden, the flaming sword
waits like a vengeful flower.
You never speak of this.
You have come like a weeping mother,
though tears do not flow.
There are rumors that the diamonds
hidden here and there
are your old tears, transformed,
though of this you never speak.
When he stoops to pluck up a rock,
you don't wince.
He stands there, one arm extends
a hug, the other sags with guilt.
You accept what is:
The past mulches under his feet,
the future grows on his face
and the present stretches in the lungs,
though he hardly breathes
for wonder of you
and what he must do.

PARABLE OF THE FISH

It was weeks before the student saw
what Agassiz said
about the fish. Not until his hands stunk
and clouds drifted
no longer in eyes relentlessly staring,
and he held the stiff,
bent tail
suspended in the next wash of ocean
when the change came—
which was
not the pale belly become more pale, though
it did, nor how pulpy the thing got
till scales came away
with the fingers,
but the new music
inside him,
like the deep rolling of water,
and the spontaneous twitch of his spine—
the breeze stirring
the stir of waves.

IN THE CELLAR

I'm standing in the cellar, the only place I smoke
inside the house, a book in one hand, the other
flicking ash into the empty pickle jar that serves

as ashtray atop a simple table of boards and
sawhorse along with the miterbox, an unopened
package of wood shims, and an old news magazine

folded over on an article about how to fix
the war in Iraq, a bare lightbulb overhead, its
pull-string dangling by my shoulder like some

lesson in planetary physics, body magnetism, or
the powerlessness of words, while exhaled smoke
invades cobwebs in the floor joists above me,

some Southern Pine, still blond, well dried,
aligned in sturdy formation that pleases
something vague in us. Did I mention it's almost

midnight and I've just come out of the bath
and stand naked in a basement, putting out
my cigarette and closing a book of poems?

MAY 31, 2008

A bus arrives at the Guard Base and
two dozen soldiers emerge into
a cloud of cheers and hysterical flags.
Wives and mothers weep. Children
leap onto striped arms heavy
with experience. Even the parents
of the dead are here, standing straight,
waving their small flags for the larger
family. The high school band is all Stars
and Stripes. The old American Legion
boys are here, at attention, saluting.
The mayor is smiles and handshakes.
It is a good day. And the war goes on.

MAPPING THE HEART

He let her long, delicate fingers go
when she told him she didn't love him anymore.
They were fourteen. He said nothing, watched
her walk home through tightening dark.
In the Greek myths, no one walked away from love.
Women died, starving horribly, dagger in the throat,
bound and dragged, wailing into slavery.
Men drank sea water, swallowed rocks, bled in battle.
He walked the streets and alleys,
brick and cement, sidewalk and litter,
each block purging their secret kisses,
each turned corner a healing scar on the heart.

BAD DAY

Driving through the city you notice
a hearse behind you.
Block after block,
the hearse is behind you.
You turn right on Appleton
and the hearse follows.
Turn left onto Beech
and the hearse follows.
You grow nervous, remember tombstone epitaphs:
  Here lies One whose name was writ in water
  Called Back
  Horseman, pass by
You slow for the red light at the next block.
It turns green before you get there
and as you enter the intersection
you see a large truck didn't stop,
misses you,
T-bones the hearse,
ripping its side,
and the coffin bounces on asphalt,
the lid breaking open,
the body flying to the sidewalk,
dying a second time.

2

APPROACHING HARVEST

When winds rush around here, searching
for unaccountable children, or a better
place to be, as if desires were tangible,
hidden around the next corner, or behind
those trees, branches surging and falling,
then the dull undersides of leaves twist
to sun side at last. The squash in the garden
huddle with fears of impermanence; bean
plants lie down in furrows, submissive,
docile as old cows. I sit atop the worn
wood table beneath the oak of those
lopped off limb tips like another
victim of this place, one more thing
that will not survive the season.

THE PROMISE OF SONG

This afternoon the first robins
stood in a circle of lawn
snow-hidden since October.
Their rapid, humid breath
melts more snow than
tonight's frigid moon
could freeze. Next week
birdsong will fill the valley.
But now someone walks
the still white field,
his heavy boots crunch
the snow with February's
only song, moonglow on
his shoulders like epaulets,
like winter's ghostly uniform
that all must wear a little longer.

BEACHED WHALE

1.

There are clouds the color of whales.
Huge masses of storm diving for dry land
to unleash a dream lost on the changed
and changing earth. Water once mated
with sky repeatedly and their splashing love,
like the trapped laughter of echoes,
touched each thing, restless or still,
and even the rocky cliffs spilled their destiny.
There are huge lungs swollen, like clouds,
in unsteady air that must always be ready,
always, for the choked gulp against
the desperate dive.

2.

The flat expanses withhold
distance. Mountains are rooted
in time. Space clots between
all things, except what hangs
in water, adjusting
to currents, to the delicacies
of light bent and diffused
in the deep
meditations of oceans
as they caress the children
with the only maternity
they need.

3.

Enmeshed in the sluice of joy along its sides,
in the rhythmic arching of rippling spines,
in the uttered voice of liquid song
that enchants the distant and draws love
near, sensation is whole, and yet
is never enough. The old whales submit
and seek the tender bottom with shut eyes
to dream of finger bones cloistered in skin,
of touch forsaken in need for steerage,
where the only link is lost forever
as waves whisper its spell: Let go.
Let go the burden. Let go the air.

4.

The liquid way to heaven
is descent. Surfacing
knifes the conscience
till memory swells like lungs
and air's sweet hypnosis
tempts no more dives. Gulls
dip and swerve in hollow
blasphemy. Ships tend
their heavy deceit. Two worlds
rupture whales. Two
mothers claim one child.
Wisdom is a gambit.

5.

And this beached whale, who bet on whiffling air
that grows bitter each new hour of exposure as sand
grubs against the thick skin, risked it all on land, on air.
The sun has no use for your kind, will lick you hard
as a rock or a road. The tide withdraws again,
snatching what it can. You stay on the shore, a lump,
an easy question for scientists and children.
Human fingers loosely rub your hide and slosh
your back with sea water, as if to clear your head.
Air will soon be done with you. We will open
a door in your side and empty you like a closet
full of clues to our own death.

SONG OF THE COMING AND GOING

Come away as rocks harden
and gases spew an atmosphere.
Come, before it is too late to rise
beyond ourselves, vaporish,
into still purposeless winds,
into the light of thought
before gravity binds us here.

Rains will come with dark contradictions
of growth and green. Soil waits its turn
as leaf-mold becomes its dream
and only crows will learn joy
in suffering dampness and fog,
their wings inhabiting the soggy spaces,
their need that great.

In the spring of what will be
grass spreads across the drying plains
and everywhere hooves touch ground
from the chase or the constant
wary search, grass will submit, will bend,
then return to the direction of sun,
to the burden it offers a world.

And when the stars fade in dirty clouds
their glint will catch
on the ripple's inner curve,
will be breathed deep within
as that last wave passes,
and no one will know the light was ours,
that we were here and left.

PRAYER IN AUTUMN

The air leans toward winter,
grass bows to approaching dusk,
wind, in its simplicity, lifts
and twists dried leaves,
a metastasis in twilight
where motions demand
attention, even when frivolous.
The slow changes go unnoticed
like the awkwardness of time
when none is left for digging
among roots, the ground hardening
from the outside in. What good
is it to know the names of leaves
when they pile like guilts
before the absolution of snow?
Lips crack in halted penance.
Everything seen in the low light
of October turns back on us.
Like a priest without conviction
the last rose falls. All winter
I face the sterile halls.

EARLY ICE

Already the Oxbow begins to freeze
along the shore, just a thin crust
of translucent, sun-shimmering ice, for now.

Think of the small pan fish
and minnows starting
to swim in widening arcs as more and more join
this dance to descend
to the deep pools that won't freeze,
and where bass and pike celebrate their arrival.

Think of frogs and salamanders
slowly adjusting their blood, their flesh,
and burrowing into the muddy bed
down below—
the last thing they do
is shut their eyes to the world.

NARRATING THE POND'S NIGHT

1. EXPOSITION

Finches and sparrows go silent,
seeking a safe perch to sway the night,
to settle in dreams of walking the earth.
Bass erupt from deep quiet
like sudden births.
Night builds a wall around
the forest pond.
A fire will not do.
I stand on the weed throttled shore.
Water licks my sneakers and the bony flesh inside.

2. COMPLICATION

Blind roots turn from bedrock, inching
in the tight earth far below
as I balance
for dry air
on a sinking rock
and fish with fake bait.

Night is a simple mouth admitting all.
Occlusions open. I detect
the song of the unmated crickets.
A toad clings like a spent star to the frail branch
falling to the water.

A bat with fur rough as the dried scales of fish
acrobats in and out of sight.

Small fish prepare for shadows on water
and the moon's cold slice into water.
I hook a bass, his buoyed meditation
snapped by the plug's burbling motion.
He whips the air a moment,
then dives, uncomprehending, for the bottom's
familiar clutch. Though he knows
how the moon chases the sun,
and the changing pressure of storms,
what I have done
is beyond him.

The abrupt suck of weeded water
when I lift the bass to air
is the only cry.
The shore conducts the cry along its edge
to infest the trees to proffer the sky
where all share
the weight of one lone thing
almost freed.

3. CLIMAX

With gill and jaw clamped in pincer fingers,
I take back the barbs
with only a slight tear
to his new burden of gravity.
I raise him to my face,
count the circles in his one, concentric eye,
and sniff the death sprouting under his fins.
I splash the bass back to renew what watery dance

is left him,
the black mirrored surface of the pond
shatters.

4. Denouement

When water gathers again its silence,
I pack my tackle. A flame shakes in threatening rain.
I turn from the shore to the scrub-choked path.
Darkness has swallowed
the human way out.

TROUBLED

The way the clouds block then funnel
the moon's light so that it splays upward
like a fan in a goddess's hand. Her
modest wind keeps mosquitoes at bay.
But we know how fickle she is, hovering
there in the southwestern sky, guardian
and trouble maker. A storm brewing.
All night rains disturb the earth. The deer
huddle beneath trees, their breath rapid,
visible. Thunder and lightning in their eyes.
Omens in my wife's waking dreams.

TWO VIEWS OF THE APOCALYPSE

1. BOULDER

The endless inching forward and back,
frozen waves of glacier along my flank,
smooth, yet cold, so smooth and cold,
then earth-warmed at last, earth-hugged
with the touch of mother come back,
and the silence doing for father,
here, secret in the earth's skin, here
I go about my business, the thick
darkness of my heart unequaled,
the dreams hard, hard and constant
as the slow voice weighted in refrain
of patience, patience, while all that time
bubbles of air were trapped between grains
of stone, trapped in contradiction of escape,
its undetectable shift deep within,
a whiff of struggle, the drowning,
choked with stillness and too much
weight grinding down dates: This
is the burden I carry to the next
inch, and the end to be.

2. Pebble

To be submerged,
stream slick,
polished and bedded down
until the flood surge of discontent
washes the banks
in annual rite,
in the wish
for the fish nudge,
in its wake of birth
and the chance to flow
downstream
where all things await,
half of me
shines like a jewel,
a moon in any weather,
a charm for the taking,
half of me shining,
and I know
my unturned side
is just as bright.

STRAIGHT LINES

They have bulldozed
a hundred mile straight line
across Africa's Navarre
to search for oil from satellite.

Except for what is made by man,
there are no straight lines
in Africa, not in river, tree trunk
or stare of lion.

Yet we love straight lines,
build with them, parade or wait
in them, type and measure them;
the mind marks them on this world.

When the Cobb antelope
reach the straight line carved perpendicular
to the migration route,
they leap across it, observers say,

as if afraid.

WINTER TEMPERATURES

Tonight in New England it is only zero,
again. Cold enough to dream of death
in the blue-black hours when nothing stirs,
when even the snowy owl hides in a tree
and wraps a wing around its eyes,
so that a rabbit can enter the white field
where a few stalks of half-seeded rye bow
from out the snow to the moon, whose slim
light hangs in air against gravity to play
with hungers, to tease the blood into
happiness, even if only for the time it takes
a small tongue to savor a small seed,
because the little rustling noise of those
few rye stems fattens across the frozen
nothingness and awakens the owl.
Later, snow will dilute the deep, deep red
spilled on its icy crust and a softened stain
will match the sky's aurora of light just
before the sun lifts over the yet dark forest.

DANCE OF THE NIGHT HAWKS

Night hawks circle above the pond.
late August; early evening; darkness
falls from trees to the earth
and slowly funnels the sky.

The hawks slip on angled wings
and dive and rise then flutter
the air, plucking insects out
the common element. Their dance
fills and empties the sky.

The only way to see the prey is
in the amplified flight of these
silhouettes of useful death.
They work and sing their song.

Night arches above us. Light
narrows like the smoke-hole
of a thatched hut. The hawks
vanish in maturing black.
But I hear that porous song

and know the dance goes on.

3

ADAM, RETURNING

What we have lost
will always be known.
Have you heard the grandchildren whispering?
We have journeyed far from them
to return today.
Look at this place!
How it has changed.
Are you sure this is it?
Where it all began?
Breathe in! Roses no longer sweeten this air.
Yes, I, too, can feel this ground
aching in my soul.
This is the place.
How heavily we walk here now.
It seems lifetimes ago
that we drifted in flowers' radiance
and couldn't resist
simply bending to touch
nose to blossom, to cup in uncalloused hands
the pure light of their color.

When last night's moon held above the horizon
and you stood beneath it,
I remembered that time in this garden:
You dressed in pink and white petals,
a garland each for hair, neck, waist.
You danced for me
and sang that song you used to know.
Remember how you took my hand
and led me to your favorite flowering bush

where we stayed the night
steeped in a fragrance gone forever?
Who can be so frivolous these days.

Here, now, we are near
that tall tree of our burden.
And that bush of yours is somewhere by,
though weeds and briars rule,
a wild thicket, as unrecognizable
as the heart of our first son.
The soil, this same soil that nurtured us
has new growth. Suspicion
sleeps securely at wisdom's gate.

Though your beguiling smile
faded, yet returns like mist to fade again,
there is still a touch of grace
as you step among this choked greenery.
And how it coaxes me.
Was it in some other life
that this tree bloomed with secrets
and your rose sweet skin
bled not?
Make it a dream, what we once had here,
a balm to ease the loss,
a shield for me
to avert that look in your eyes
I've seen before.
Do not do this, my fateful one.
Must I taste all again.

HISTORY AND OXYMORONS

Hammurabi said some things about
stolen oxen and ownership. He was a wise

man who lived almost exactly
at the inception of civilization.

When he died, silent screams exploded
the common palace walls. The voiceless wailing

of the small crowd that gathered then
dispersed when the winds came pelting

desert sands with a pretty ugly force.
The one entrusted with the tablets

of Hammurabi's words let them fall to take
his child's hand. Everything shattered

like bird eggs acting out the nature of gravity
and ideas. Whole fragments scattered

throughout the land so that the unruly
people in the next valley began to plot

an exact estimate of how long it would take
government to spread like so many grains

of sand because there are so many quarrels
over oxen and brides and spilled blood.

HAMLET AS ANTHROAPOLOGIST

Even if we look for Ophelia in the violets,
and clip the budded stems to color
the empty evenings, it is not love.
From flower to loam, from flesh to bone,
the stones we dig are skulls.
We count them, varnish them
with the care of a cosmetologist
and stack them on shelves labeled
Cleopatra, Venus of Trier, Ann Bradstreet.
We will charge the unsuspecting dollars
to witness this spectacle of death.
This is how we change the past
and rewrite the future. These skulls,
we love them because they are not us.

MOLASSES COOKIES

No mother could count her sons
dying in war like leaves falling
from the tree in the front yard.
Nor could she say the names of where,
though the father did, until those
angry places became a litany,
their vowels scrying through kitchen,
consonants plaguing the heaving air
of parlor and bedroom. She heard
the wind in the tree bleed *Saipan*.
All night the radiator
knocked *Remachen. Remachen.*
In the morning the telephone
cried *Anzio.* She heard them
everywhere, memorized them
and fed the fear of cursing
the last boy still breathing out there
somewhere beyond the dark waters.
Each week she bakes molasses cookies,
wraps and boxes them, writes a boy's name
on the label, mails them overseas to
William Enright, Jr., Jonathan Jones,
Walter Fondolowski, Eddie Burlon-Smith,
names in her imagination,
someone's boys over there huddled
in night who will open the package,
remember home, the aroma
of pot roast, the whiteness of doilies,
lace curtains tied back just so.

AT THE NURSING HOME

She visits you every day,
says she is your daughter.
You nod, politely,

wishing she'd leave
before she tells more stories
of people you don't know.

Your memories are
tissues crumpled
in a wastebasket.

The bird at the window
is your youngest
born in a snowstorm.

Photos on the mantle
around you close like doors
that never open again.

THIS LIFE

Where the children's feet scraped
away the grass beneath the swings
in the park, one tall puffball
stands at grass's edge, hardy,
stubborn weed only a child
could love, like some old man
in the cancer ward refusing
as long as he can to give up
his place to the next generation
so that all the white-coated
doctors, male and female,
shake their heads at him,
unable to understand the need
to wait for the right moment,
like the puffball in the park
that needs the west wind
and no other to blow it apart,
to carry each dark seed
under its white sail across
the field to where the soil is
damp and warm and welcoming,
like the child crawling onto
grandpa's hospital bed
and withered arms
take up the child and a hoarse
voice announces to everyone
in that small, pale room,
"If I embrace this life,
I do not die."

HIV

The lab report
on the desk,

a doctor stares
at the telephone—

your number
in her hand.

THE GIRL ON THE COVER OF THE MAGAZINE

sits on the sad floor
with legs pulled up against her body.
Arms gently crossed atop her knees.
Her head lowered, secretly
reading the history of her wrists.

Her hair weeps darkly down back,
her shoulders, and one elbow.
The crinkled skirt splays around her
like the after urge of ebb tide.

The toes of her right foot risk everything
to breathe in unencumbered air.
When she rises, she will take
the long way home, inhaling deeply
to fill vacant spaces within.

If a bird sings, she will not hear it.
If a few drops of rain splash the sidewalk,
her bare feet will neither smile nor frown.
If a car's horn breaks the air,
it's all one to her.

One foot, then another.
One step at a time is what it takes
to carve a path over the mountain
to the valley.

A HOUSE WITHOUT CHICKEN

A house without chicken means
no soup on winter weekends simmering
on stove top so that the whole, closed-in
house fills with aromas, and coming in
from the frigid outside, you could eat
the very air of the kitchen, then sit
with a book, sated with flavors and words.
But not today, when the snow is stale
and the pale walls lack color or fragrance.
It might as well be the dead of night
where bodies dream senselessly under
comforters plied atop skin and bones
for all the lack of seasoning in their lives.

MODERN FARM

In a little while these field
feeding cows will be led
to the high tech barn
where the chrome machines
suck them dry.

Weathered barn board
decorates walls in houses
built on the pastures
of the bankrupt neighbor farm
whose metal milk cans,
full of soil and flowers,
shine on the new stairs.

The sound of the eighteen wheeler
from the co-op shifts down
the mountain road
in the distance.

It will take the white gold
and leave dust in its wake.

ANONYMOUS DONATION

It got to twenty-seven below that winter,
which is harsh for Massachusetts,
even as far west as the hills near Pittsfield.

I mixed stucco that week, by hand.
The mixing bed was splashed with ice.
We set it on the cement floor of a large box.

The box became a luxury condominium.
With every third pull of the hoe, I rested,
to let the lungs thaw, to exhale a cloud

and waste a moment watching my crystal breath.
Such scenery would never be framed
and hung on these walls when finished.

So I mixed it into the stucco.
And quit the job.

LINT

It doesn't bother me to have
lint in the bottoms of pant pockets;
it gives the hands something to do,
especially since I no longer hold
shovel, hod or hammer
in the daylight hours of labor
and haven't, in fact, done so
in fifty-five years. A long time
to be picking lint from pockets.
Perhaps even long enough to have
gathered sacks full of lint
that could have been put
to good use, maybe spun into yarn
to knit a sweater for my wife's
Christmas present, or strong thread
woven into a tweedy jacket.
Imagine entering my classroom
in a jacket made from lint.
Who would believe it?
Yet there are stranger things—
the son of a bricklayer with hands
so smooth they're only fit
for picking lint.

4

THE WINE GLASS

Eyes in the crowd touch
and two strangers suddenly believe
they are secret lovers

. . .they sit at a table on a sidewalk
in Luxembourg, their voices a murmur;
sunlight plays with the glass, the wine;
he smiles at the skin on her neck,
smooth and curving as the wine glass
and touches the hem of her skirt;
she raises the glass to her lips,
gives him that look he always loves
and leans toward him. . .

but the sidewalk under their feet
is hard and cold and they pass each other
intimate strangers.

CONCERTO FOR LOVE: A NIGHT PIECE

1.

The crickets again. Their song rattled
the bedroom and the bones in the bedroom.
Nights of summer, nights of absences.
The tempo of sleep, of love, or the lack
of love, drifted, lost in the haze
of overture. Darkness rushed through
the background like kettledrums. The oaks:
whorled as air held too long in lungs.
Tree toads made the chorus; everyone of them
a prince; each one hidden in the din of voices.
The waltz stepped in and out the ears.
The arms emptied. Air grew thick.
Upright, a body stumbled across the floor.
The hands played the black keys from memory.

2.

Music and love searched the corners,
needing to be complete. Silence sat there.
Dream twisted into other notes. Awake
was its own nightmare. There was no
applause. The black drunk of night.
Demands like moths clinging to underleafs.
The catbird sang the climax, a rehearsed numbness
of hollow bones, a horn choked with breath.
There is only one theme. Always the dual
desire. The doorway that divorced itself
from night stood by the bed. Damp air
from the open window. Curtains swaying.
Then the wings of bats, like old babies, clapping.

A SUMMARY OF LOVE LETTERS
NEVER MAILED

Each time the words began to flow
as if waves chewed the moonless shore
at an endless bitter supper.
The heart beat like tree-bound birds
eyeing the wet shore littered with shells
the minute before the sun lifts into view.

Each time those words warped
like the legs of cranes flocking overhead
with illegible omen, and the promised
change in season blurred as feathers lost
at lift-off and tattering in winds of storm
not even this poem can shape.

THE GHOST OF LOVE: A VALENTINE OF LOSS

i.

The blue light in the midnight fist of Orion
slipped through the obscure distance
and splashed upon another hunter
stumbling along a lonely pond, water of life, water of lust
and love, bounded by dark fauna, darker stone.
Though he tried his best to capture love,
to capture and consecrate love,
beasts roamed the wilderness, their blessings
or burdens suspended in snared breath.
Night, too, withheld its screams.
Something more was expected to stir the air.
He sat at pond's edge
still as a moon-moth sniffing the blind air,
faint light loose around his hands.
The breeze that moaned in pine trees
and lapped bright jewels of water on shored rocks
died in his seiney arms.

ii.

For lost love he stayed with the night silence of water
without even a whisper
of her beauty, of her voice fading like the angels of childhood,
and he choked on the depth
of an unsounded lump in the throat,
the moonless agitation attending
the lost granite gripping the shoreline, its knowledge of day
forgotten in fallen height,
as rock preached to them

its cold sermon
so that now, at last, under dimmed clouds,
in the mirrored blue-blackness,
with love a dying flame,
the difference between stone and water and flesh
resolved in black similitude.

iii.

Her ghost slipped from his side, willow-thin, wispy
as exhaled air, and he tried to breathe her in,
hold her like a word along the bronchial cilla,
but she began to dance across
the dark water in ritual delight, danced
beyond the shore-hemmed soul abandoned to marry blackness,
danced beyond the teasing reach of anything human,
so that the joining of myth and man,
like cloud and sky, field and flower, grape and vine,
the blessed binding into one new creature
shuddered, faltered as spokes shattering within the wheel,
its sonorous repetition imploding in failed rhythm,
in the music and dance that loses at first its sweetness
before vinegar splatters against the heart. Such
was that dance: lovely and chilly,
excitement and delusion.

iv.

A bullfrog cracked the deep still to proclaim the hour was its.
Pine boughs mourned their containment.
Crickets applauded from every sudden where.
She sang or hummed, he couldn't tell, but he knew

deep in marrow that harmony—more superior than dream,
with a promise as full as white and purple
lavender swaying, purity and blood,
completing the sweet air
of imagined spring,
and the song sluiced the black from out the air
so that a thrill of stars shone
in her eyes while waves glowed with rippled
tears across his cheeks, a pink suggestion
fading into the vanishing point of night's heavy canvas
stretched across the nightmare
kept hidden until
the final, awful truth clicked
with dream and hope's
evaporation.

V.

He rose from the tree-shouldered shore,
an Orion loosened from the elliptic, roused, almost gladdened,
and primed, but without new challenge.
He reached out to her withs hands of vapor, fingers
a mist of nothing, less than air,
the bread of his heart
disassembling in the dismal water.
Some fish, twitching with instinct, some opportunistic bass
that only acknowledges hunger in pantheonless existence,
splashed skyward to feed, its mouth drooling
night's urgency as it swallowed a moth like an angel.
He stood in the joyless air and claimed as legacy
this moment, this mountain of sorrow
that neither wind nor rain nor ice could weather

or reduce to the dust gelling in his veins
and spreading like false light.
And when the moon rose at last,
when it finally blossomed into consciousness,
it thrashed the diluted weight of its shining against horizons
without mercy for granite or passion.

ISLANDS OF FAREWELL

"The sun for sorrow will not show his head"
—*Romeo & Juliet*, V, iii, 306

"They left/me clutching/islands of farewell"
—Agha Shahid Ali

The night's horizonal glow
is the crack of light
from behind the world's locked door.
Whatever keys there were are lost.
Someone could say
to the blank dark, "Love
was the purpose, the promise...."
But a cut rose is just
a dead vegetable rotting the water.
A sweet name can sweeten
the bitter imagination
just so long before the shoulder,
smashing against the denied door,
separates, and the pain, oh the pain,
is the ticket to the emergency room
whose automatic doors
open for everyone.
Here the light is cold.
Here the smiles are rare and sardonic.
Someone could whisper
in the smelly hospital corridor,
"Sarcoma." Faces will turn
and walk away. A body will struggle
in damp sheets because it can not find
the light at the end of the tunnel.
And because the throat is tumorous
beyond speech, it can not tell us
the truth. Or even a lie.

THE LAST CHILDHOOD HERO

Father, that time
in the hospital, tubes
in both your nostrils, the machine
pumped noise and life
by the bed, like a delirious angel
trying to reconstruct
the fluids of your ruptured stomach
and the too much drink.
Your foul blood
was hung in a plastic bag
to exhibit the sin.
They didn't bother with mopping your brow.
You sweat like a prisoner,
a martyr, fate uncertain,
with nothing to do
but submit
to strange hands
forcing life back in.
I stood there, a mute exclamation,
staring at the withered body of just
another man,
defrocked at last.

LOVE: THE UNSPOKEN

There are no names for the ache
standing behind her at the sink,
kneading her spine with specter hands,
massaging silence into the marrow.
The dishes are done in the wordless care
of altar pieces. Her fingers
riffle in wash water like vocal cords
twisted and wrenched in a vacuum
where speech decomposed in hush.
The diaper pail squats in the corner,
clean as a gilded dome.
The nipple leaked for two years after
the baby's birth, the call
to motherhood a soured generosity.
Her soft humming makes the only sense.
Cobwebs reappear where walls meet
in another routine of silence
to gather in rags, to loosen
in winds, like all the stilled dreams.
Humming only endures, like heart
beats in the death of sleep
where the unspoken is pumped into
mute arteries, into love.

AN OLD STORY

A girl leaves her father's house and leaps into
the boy's boat to sail to the horizon. It could be
the South Pacific or the Cyclades Islands. But this
is an old story. Like the day I cashed in my pilot
training money to buy Natalie, an ocean away,
a diamond ring, the longing greater than the dream.
And when my niece announced she and he were
eloping to Vegas, they invited us into Nevada heat.
How perfect for them, no longer kids, to pretend
to run away. And how perfect for us to join in
their adventure. And when my daughter's guy
showed me, after Easter dinner, the ring he bought
for her then asked permission, I thought how odd,
how old fashioned, how proper, this boy raised
in Florida. I remember his surprise when
I hugged him, just so he'd know whom he was
dealing with, and said directly in his ear, all I ask
is that you truly love her. And all this comes
to mind today because, as soon as the fog lifted
off the beach in Dennisport, Cape Cod, a single
engine airplane flew overhead trailing a banner
that said: *Liz will you marry me* ❤ *Geoff.* No one
there knew Liz or Geoff, so everyone searched
up and down the sand for a couple embracing,
or a woman leaping and waving. And why
shouldn't she. Sweet and daring and so public
a request. Each wanted to be first to spot Liz as if
finding her was to share in her joy, if there was
joy. But there wasn't. There were only sun bathers
looking left, right, then up as the plane circled back,

then again, rocking its wings this time to draw
attention, as if that banner, itself, that declaration
flapping in air above us was not enough, that
words, alone, are never enough.

VANISHING POINT

Staring, you look for clues.
Where is the evidence, the proof.

In your stare I watch myself gazing,
enamored at skylines,
or blinded by a pine cone in hand.

Love, when it stays, is traceless.
Whose hand stretched first offering is no matter.
The bodies press together in their many ways.

The one coarse piece of cloth drapes us both
and softens on our curves so our lives fit well.

When two people journey far enough into the distance
they merge.

FIRST SPRING
(for Nadia)

Green touched the winter view
and fits of snow dusted the scene
one last white time.
I held you to the window
but the grass and crocus bursting colors
were too distant.

Outside your unsure steps took
the urgency of light
and tottered toward some celebration
more felt than known.
Only the first and last steps,
like the leaves on New England trees,
are worth counting.
I gathered the thin snow in my palm,
a bouquet of frozen years.
You blew the white petals into my face
and laughed.

In another place or time
this might be ritual.
Father brings daughter to a threshold,
unfurls the paths to choose,
then counts her footsteps
and marks this first moment
she walks alone
into spring light and doesn't
look back.

THE BIRTH

(for Jason)

1.

First Easter. And then
you were born
as if to prove a point. Snow
still whispered its hardships under yews.
The sacrifice of flowers
lit the ward room
where wife and husband bordered
on mother and father. We looked
to the corners as if a lost thing
huddled there,
the changed views
trapped in the altercation of seasons.
I hold no mystery in the blue of robin eggs
or the birth sacks of cats,
but just born hands, lined with perfection,
grasp at something we don't yet know.

2.

There were whispers in the nightdeep hospital air
that tangled her hair, stammered talk
of a small life squeezed out after hours of struggle,
of how you were stubborn
from the start, refusing to share our light,
the air touching the first visible you
like nothing kind.
I know winds that tease with sudden calm,
each pause a surprise
like a message remembered too late.

The world was determined
to have you,
though machines couldn't yank
you out like a tulip bulb,
as you came,
breached, legs
bent to the head like some acrobat
caught in mid
performance, and left to a sense of balance
dangling on an inner clock.
You couldn't get back
so you soiled the doctor's hands
and ripped your mother's skin.
They doped her near the end,
then sewed her up, neat,
an extra stitch
and good as new.
It must be then the cold antiseptic hands
carried you, like an offering, to the scales
and laid you out for measuring,
all purple and white
as if you entered life dressed
for resurrection.

3.
A rumored life and death
is made ritual,
the sepulcher locked in the weight of belief,
then opened, empty except for genuflected awe
withered in rehearsed mystery.
The promises bloom

only to shed like forsythia,
the blooming bush
changing color and scent.
For three days I journeyed to her
as if to a shrine: Flowers, chocolates,
teddy bear and empty aching arms.
It is the child who speaks to my future.
And coming on the tears of the Virgin,
the child is full of little dooms
and triumphs
even before he begins.

ENGINEERING SWEET DREAMS

(for Piper)

So I ate my son-in-law's mint
chocolate after a cigarette.
It was the last one. He will not
be pleased, but won't say so.
I let the chocolate sit on the tongue,
slowly vanishing the way morning fog
slips between trees and is gone,
until all that remains is a memory
made sweet by the play of sunlight
and shadow, or the way saying
'I love you' disappears into a kiss.
But what else could I do—
it was time to give my granddaughter
her noon bottle. When I snuggle
and feed her, do you think she wants
stale tobacco on my breath,
or the aroma of chocolate?
She doesn't know either, but we
want her dreams to be sweet.

ABOUT THE AUTHOR

 GARY METRAS is the author of eight books of poetry along with thirteen chapbooks. His *White Storm* (Presa Press, 2018) was selected as a Must Read title in the Massachusetts Books of the Year Program. His essays, reviews, and chiefly poems have appeared in hundreds of journals and anthologies since the 1970s, including *America, American Life in Poetry, Boston Review of Books, California Quarterly, The Common, Connecticut Poetry Review, Gray's Sporting Journal, Hawai'i Pacific Review, New England Watershed, North Dakota Quarterly, Poetry, Poetry East, Poetry Salzburg Review, San Antonio Review, Santa Fe Literary Review, South Florida Poetry Journal, Tears in the Fence,* (UK) and *Visiting Frost: Poems Inspired by the Life and Work of Robert Frost* (Iowa). A master letterpress printer, he founded and edited Adastra Press for forty years, releasing numerous fine press poetry limited editions. He lives in Easthampton, Massachusetts, where, in April 2018, he was appointed as the city's inaugural Poet Laureate.